REAGANCOMICS

A Cornucopia of Cartoons
on Ronald Reagan

FOREWORD BY MORLEY SAFER
INTRODUCTION BY RALPH NADER

KHYBER PRESS PUBLICATIONS • SEATTLE

Published by Khyber Press
P. O. Box 1616
Auburn, Washington

ISBN 0-9611396-1-7

Library of Congress Catalog Number: 84-080935

Printed in the United States of America

Printer: Delta Lithograph Company, Van Nuys, California

Distributor: Publishers Group West, Emeryville, California

Cover Artist: David Horsey, Editorial Cartoonist,
Seattle Post-Intelligencer, Seattle, Washington

Cover Designer: Tom Schworer, Seattle, Washington

Front Cover: Our apologies to Dorothy, the Lion, the
Scarecrow, the Tin Man, Toto, and some fellow by the
name of Frank L. Baum.

"Acting is the art of speaking in a loud clear voice and the avoidance of bumping into furniture."

—*Alfred Lunt*

Foreword

The great advantage that the editorial cartoonist has over the editorial writer is that he is not restricted by the canons of good taste, or at least not by what is perceived as good taste in the funereal corridors of most newspaper offices.

Editorial cartoonists are, generally speaking, the loose cannons of the newsroom. In one breath they are the hardhats, in another they are the bleeding hearts, and in yet another—on their really good days—they are the Swifts and Daumiers of their time . . . skewering rascals, cocking a snook at the blowhards of politics, or planting a swift kick in the soft underbelly of society.

This book chooses a single target—a beaut . . . Ronald Wilson Reagan. It is definitely not true that the 1980 election was rigged by the country's cartoonists who had burnt themselves out in the course of burning out Jimmy Carter. Americans are quite capable of electing men like Carter and Reagan all by themselves . . . Thank goodness. Without such men and their tormentors, all editorial pages would look like those of the *New York Times*. The *Times,* which does not carry political cartoons, prints an editorial page that has all the wit of a timetable for the Long Island Railway. People have been known to die of solemnity while reading the *Times'* editorials.

The value of the editorial cartoonist lies in his inability to be fair. Subversion is his game. His pen is jaundiced. He rarely has anything nice to say in his wonderful space. You may see Ronald Reagan as the Great Communicator, the avuncular cowboy, or the Virtuous Leader of the Free World. A cartoonist, however, sees a geriatric, slightly deaf codger with turkey wattles, whose finger is on the nuclear button and whose brain is on the F.B.I.'s Missing Persons List. No offence, of course. Ronald Reagan simply has the misfortune of being president of the United States, and the cartoonist is only doing his job.

Reporters report. For better or worse, we are the grunts of the news wars.

Columnists take postures. They are the beauty queens, the prize heifers of the newsroom. You know that you are reading a column when you give up after the second sentence. I offer two exceptions, Russell Baker of the *New York Times* and Calvin Trillin of the *Nation*. Both are subversives who doubt everything, particularly what they read in the newspapers. If they could draw, they would be cartoonists.

Editorial writers smoke pipes and think about their pensions. Sometimes they write. But mostly they just type.

Cartoonists, however, do what they do in the fewest possible words and in the least amount of space. The line in India ink can be as pure a piece of literate journalism as you will find anywhere in the paper. It is also a fuse that can detonate the mind of the reader. The effect may be laughter, but as you will see when you turn these pages, the purpose is serious.

It is not a deadly seriousness, though. America's newspapers are a glorious celebration of the liberty of this country, but they can be very dull . . . a long grey, leaden march through the lively history of our time. I often feel about them as Dr. Johnson felt about the novels of Congreve: I would rather praise them than read them. I feel exactly the opposite about the cartoons: I would rather look at them than praise them. Please feel free to do both.

Morely Safer
New York, New York
April 17, 1984

Introduction

It has been said of Ronald Reagan that he smiled, shrugged, and showboated his way from Hollywood to Sacramento to the White House. The grin, the gag, the fictional anecdote, the gaffe—all have been Mr. Reagan's stock in trade. In the year he won the governship of California from Edmund Brown, the first Democrat who underestimated him, the man from "Death Valley Days" said: "Politics is just like show business. You have a hell of an opening, coast for a while, and then have a hell of a close."

Since he became president, Mr. Reagan has confounded opponents and pundits alike with the politics of reduced expectations, the politics of "aw shucks," the politics of waving the flag and rolling with the punches, the politics of running against one's own record deficits while working the shortest days since Warren G. Harding's tenure. Former secretary of defense and veteran lawyer, Clark Clifford, once called him, at a private gathering, an "amiable dunce." It is pretty difficult to put such a personality on the defensive, as legions of Democrats are finding out.

Richard Cohen, a popular columnist with the *Washington Post,* expressed his amazement: "This president is treated by both the press and foreign leaders as if he were a child. He earns praise for the ordinary, for what used to be expected. His occasional ability to retain facts is cited as a triumph when it should, in fact, be a routine occurrence . . . ."

Indeed, who else could survive such statements as: "Those (nuclear weapons) that are carried in ships of one kind or another, or submersibles, you are dealing there with a conventional type of weapon or instrument, and those instruments can be intercepted. They can be recalled." Or, "We were told four years ago that 17 million people went to bed hungry every night. Well, that was probably true. They were all on a diet." Or, his description of Medicaid recipients: ". . . a faceless mass, waiting for handouts." Or, regarding redwoods: "A tree's a tree. How many more do you need to look at?" Or, in the mid-sixties, his comment on the emerging African nations to the effect that when those countries "have a man to lunch, they really have him to lunch." Or, "unemployment insurance is a prepaid vacation for free-loaders."

These sayings of Chairman Ron are just a few examples of the Presidential mind in the Oval Office. Those of you who wish to suffer more of the same and worse can pick up a paperback called *Ronald Reagan's Reign of Error* (Pantheon Books, N.Y.). For those citizens who like to take their tragi-comedy in short cartoon bursts, *Reagancomics* is the book to open. There is a temptation to flip through the pages of a collection of cartoons with the speed of a clicking camera. That would be a mistake here. These cartoons are best savored, even mulled over as a memory prod for the rest of the horrible iceberg. Let the wit of the cartoonist have time to illuminate your thoughts as it tickles your chuckles.

Someone once observed that "In humor there is truth." Yes, but there is also a texture of sadness. As *Reagancomics* portrays waves of abuses, national deficits, human cruelty and unfairness, laziness, insensitivity, waste, secrecy, and munitions-mania, the insightful, humorous drawings (note the one showing Reagan looking at his horse peering in the window), make the dismal messages more absorbable. It is not pleasant, after all, to see the national government of Exxon, by General Motors, and for Dupont moving relentlessly to destroy the country's crucial health and safety programs; to raise the deficit to levels three or four times that of Jimmy Carter's administration; to cut programs designed to help young students, the disabled, veterans, the poor, the elderly, consumers and workers; to transfer the riches of our public lands to mega-corporate control; to take the federal cop off the corporate beat leading to more recidivistic business crime that pollutes the air, water and soil; and to launch a budget-busting, gouging military arms procurement spree financed by small taxpayers as the rich and powerful laugh all the way to their tax shelters.

Sometimes the sheer detail of the Reagan regime can overwhelm people with the vast erosion that is taking place. Here, Reagan's calculated image-making and rhetoric move to obscure recollection of the full sweep of the wasteland he is expanding. Using soothing assurances, material omissions, and voodoo statistics, he tries to place rose-colored glasses over one hundred million television sets with his unilateral speeches to which network policies permit no rebuttal.

Cartoons are images also. However, unlike the current president, cartoons put you on guard. They neither trick nor camouflage. Rather, they wear their laughs on their sleeves. As readers turn the pages of this book to refresh their memory, the road to the ballot booth in November, 1984, may become a little more crowded. If by chance some readers don't think the picture is that bad, be patient, for what you've seen to date would be a mere glimmer should there be four more Reagan years. . . .

Ralph Nader
Washington, D.C.
April, 1984

Contributing Artists

In the making of this book, we have become reacquainted with the meaning of the word creativity—the editorial cartoonists of the United States. With each cartoon considered, our appreciation for them as artists grew. And for each time they made us laugh, our respect for their quirky sense of humor—honesty—helped us to remember the true purpose of this book.

This collection of cartoons is an historical document, the cartoonists having served as historians. Customarily it is found that the cartoons of today become the fish wrap of tomorrow. It has been our goal to prevent this particular set of cartoons from encountering this unjust demise.

Once again, our thanks.

—The Editors

Ken Alexander—San Francisco Examiner and Copley News Service

Tony Auth—Philadelphia Inquirer and Washington Post Writers Group

Chuck Ayers—Akron Beacon Journal

John Backderf—Rothco Cartoons, Inc.

Brian Basset—Seattle Times

Bruce Beattie—Daytona Beach Morning Journal

H. Clay Bennett—St. Petersburg Times

Stephen Benson—Arizona Republic and Washington Post Writers Group

Jim Berry—Newspaper Enterprise Association

Jim Borgman—Cincinnati Enquirer and King Features Syndicate, Inc.

John Branch—San Antonio Express-News

Berke Breathed—Washington Post Writers Group

Bob Englehart—Hartford Courant and Los Angeles Times Syndicate

Jules Feiffer—Universal Press Syndicate

Ed Fischer—Rochester Post-Bulletin and McNaught Syndicate, Inc.

George Fisher—Arkansas Gazette

Joseph Heller—West Bend News

David Horsey—Seattle Post-Intelligencer and Copley News Service

Etta Hulme—Fort Worth Star-Telegram and Newspaper Enterprise Association

Lee Judge—Kansas City Star and Times

Mike Keefe—Denver Post and Field Newspaper Syndicate

Mike Lane—Evening Sun Baltimore and Copley News Service

Richard Locher—Chicago Tribune and Tribune Company Syndicate

M.G. Lord—Newsday, Long Island

Jeff MacNelly—Chicago Tribune and Tribune Company Syndicate

Jimmy Margulies—Houston Post

Doug Marlette—King Features Syndicate, Inc.

Tim Menees—Pittsburgh Post-Gazette

Tom Meyer—San Francisco Chronicle

Jim Morin—Miami Herald

Jack Ohman—The Oregonian

Pat Oliphant—Universal Press Syndicate

Mike Peters—Dayton Daily News and United Feature Syndicate

Dwayne Powell—News and Observor; Los Angeles Times Syndicate

Milt Priggee—Dayton Journal Herald and Copley News Service

Sam Rawls—The Altanta Constitution and Newspaper Enterprise Association

Steve Sack—Minneapolis Star and Tribune and Tribune Company Syndicate

Ed Stein—Rocky Mountain News and Newspaper Enterprise Association

Dana Summers—Orlando Sentinel and Copley News Service

John Trever—Albuquerque Journal and Field Newspaper Syndicate

Garry Trudeau—Universal Press Syndicate

Pete Wagner—City Pages, Minneapolis

Kerry Waghorn—Chronicle Features

Signe Wilkinson—San Jose Mercury News

Scott Willis—Dallas Times Herald

Don Wright—Miami News and Tribune Company Syndicate

REAGANCOMICS

"I can't come out and play now. I've got to work for a couple of hours."

4

'OH, ME, TOO - WHY, WHEN WE'RE AT THE RANCH, I JUST LOVE CAMPING OUT !'

5

6

'OF COURSE WE CONSIDERED REAGAN'S MIDEAST PEACE PLAN-WE WROTE IT IN THE SAND HERE SOMEWHERE...'

HE'S LOST.
HE'S ALONE.
HE'S 146,000,000,000 DOLLARS
FROM A BALANCED BUDGET.
E.P.
"THE EXTRA-PREZ-ESTRIAL"
REALITY
RECOMMENDED for TRICKLE-DOWN AUDIENCES
MINNEAPOLIS STAR AND TRIBUNE

12

DAYTON
JOURNAL HERALD

13

14

©83 Daytona Beach Morning Journal

BEATTE

White House EAST ROOM

"Listen, you know the president likes to project a tough image to the Soviets...
Get him out of here before Ron makes him secretary of state!"

16

17

'AH, NOT TOO MANY, AT ALL! THAT SHOWS A DISTINCT IMPROVEMENT IN HUMAN RIGHTS, MR. SCHULTZ.'

18

21

22

OuR NuClear DeTeRRenT

So FaR, THe aRMS BuiLDuP HaS PReVeNTeD:

a FRiGHTeNiNG eScaLaTion OF SCHooL LuncHeS.

THe OMiNOUS SPeCTeR OF PooR PeoPLe GeTTiNG LeGaL aiD.

a DeSTaBiLiZiNG BuiLDuP OF THe aRTS.

THe MaSSiVe PRoLiFeRaTioN OF CoLLeGe GRaDuaTeS.

STeiN '82
ROCKY
MTN.
NEWS
NEA

23

REAGAN GUIDEBOOK FOR CIVIL DEFENSE

1. LEARNING OF AN IMMINENT ATTACK, REAGAN ASKS RUSSIA FOR ONE WEEK DELAY TO IMPLEMENT PLAN.

2. CITY DWELLERS ARE CALMLY EVACUATED TO THE COUNTRY.

"LET'S WAIT AND LET A FEW OTHERS GET IN LINE..."

3. ...AND YOUR SAME-DAY DELIVERY OF THE WALL STREET JOURNAL IS SET UP...

RURAL RESIDENTS PITCH IN TO HELP DISPLACED URBANITES.

4. BEFORE PRESSING **THE** BUTTON, BREZHNEV CHECKS WITH REAGAN TO MAKE SURE EVERYONE IS SAFE.

5. MISSILES DESTROY U.S. CITIES.

6. OUR MISSILES DESTROY RUSSIA... *WE WIN!!*

7. USING PIONEER SPIRIT, CITIES ARE RE-BUILT IN A DAY OR SO.

8. NANCY GETS NEW WHITE HOUSE FOR HER CHINA.

9. EVERYTHING IS HUNKY-DORY EVER AFTER.

LOS ANGELES TIMES SYNDICATE ©4/2/82 - THE NEWS AND OBSERVER

24

27

DOONESBURY

WHEN RONALD REAGAN TALKS...

30

News Item: Justice Dept. finds no crime when Reagan obtained Carter briefing book.

"IT'S THE NICE MAN FROM THE JOINT CHIEFS, HARVEY — HERE TO SEE ABOUT
THE **MX** BASING MODE AGAIN!"

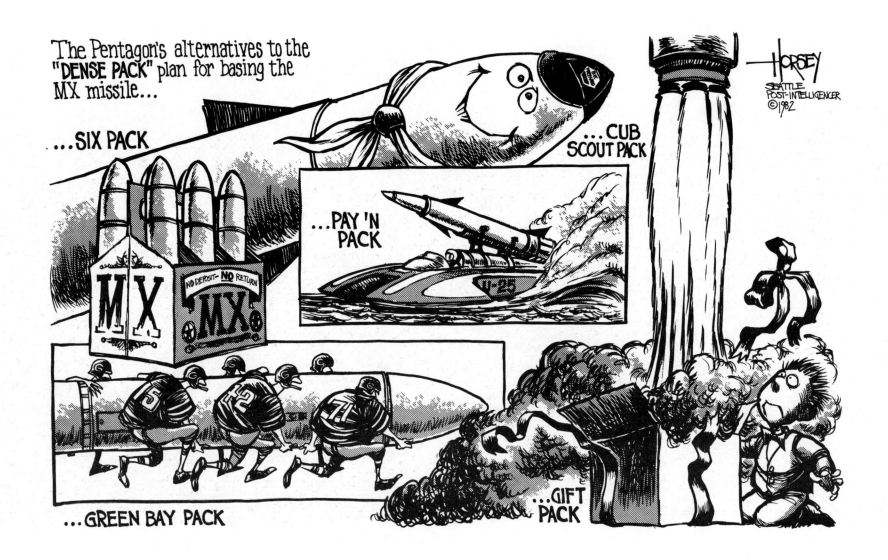

35

"THE PRESIDENT IS VERY CLOSE TO BEING IN CONCRETE IN REFUSING DEFENSE CUTS" — SENATOR LAXALT

" ...LADIES AND GENTLEMEN, THE PRESIDENT... "

41

And it disappeared
quite slowly
beginning with
its tail and ending
with its grin,
which remained
for some time

—Cheshire cat
Alice in Wonderland

Balanced Budget

ED FISCHER
ROCHESTER POST-BULLETIN

42

IF THERE'S ONE THING THAT MAKES ME REALLY ANGRY IT'S THE WAY THESE DEMOCRATS ARE SCARING OUR OLDER AMERICANS ON THE SOCIAL SECURITY ISSUE.

THEY'RE FRIGHTENING A LOT OF POOR, DEFENSELESS PEOPLE BY TELLING THEM HOW MUCH OUR $40 BILLION CUTS ARE GOING TO HURT THEM.

CALL ME A SOFTIE, BUT I JUST DON'T THINK IT'S RIGHT TO GO AROUND TERRORIZING OLD PEOPLE.

THERE THEY ARE, CRITICIZING CUTS THEY HAD NOTHING TO DO WITH AND THEY DON'T EVEN SUPPORT!

THAT REMINDS ME OF A STORY...., SEEMS THERE WAS THIS FELLA HAD TWO CHICKENS. ONE SAYS TO THE OTHER, "WHICH CAME FIRST, THE OMELET OR THE EGG?" THE OTHER ONE SAYS, "THAT'S WHY I CROSSED THE ROAD!"

WELL, THAT'S JUST LIKE THE DEMOCRATS. NOW I DON'T WANT TO BEAT A DEAD BUSH, BUT LET ME JUST SAY—

MATH BY DAVID STOCKMAN, LOGIC BY RONALD REAGAN

"That little giggle of yours is a dead giveaway that you've found MORE cuts to be made in social programs."

49

THE PRESIDENT FINALLY ACHIEVES A BIPARTISAN FOREIGN POLICY CONSENSUS ON CENTRAL AMERICA...

52

NICARAGUA ADMITTED TODAY TO THE MINING OF NEW YORK HARBOR TO FORCE THE U.S. TO CHANGE ITS GOVERNMENT TO ONE MORE ACCEPTABLE TO MANAGUA.

53

54

56

"HAVE YOU EVER THOUGHT ABOUT GETTING A NEWSPAPER ROUTE?."

58

Daily Di...

"All the news that's left"

Weather: partly ███, warmer

███ Administration Defends New Secrecy Rules

By ███ ███

WASHINGTON (███) — The ███ administration today strongly defended its secrecy in tightening of government. Administration spokesman ███ said, "We ███ deny that ███ hinder the public right to know." He added, "After all, what ███ know can't ███ them."

Members of the press, however, ███ Said ███

In th' neighb' worker found low-do Admi: becau used Bu beco Den one pay hel pay

D' at n' f: v

President ███ ...fends secrecy

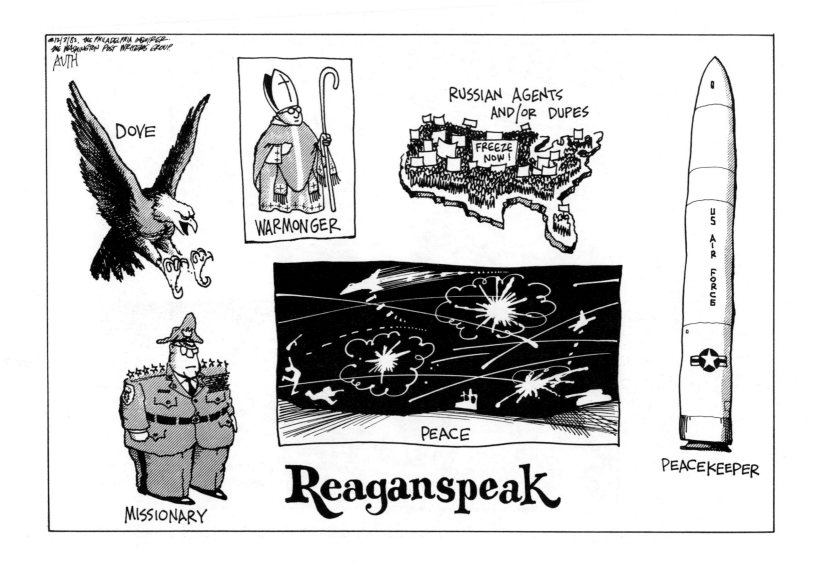

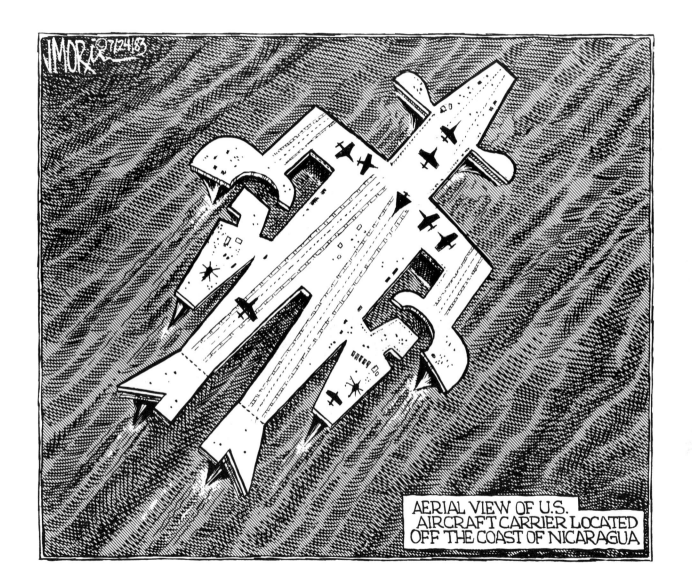

AERIAL VIEW OF U.S.
AIRCRAFT CARRIER LOCATED
OFF THE COAST OF NICARAGUA

© 1981 SAN ANTONIO EXPRESS-NEWS

67

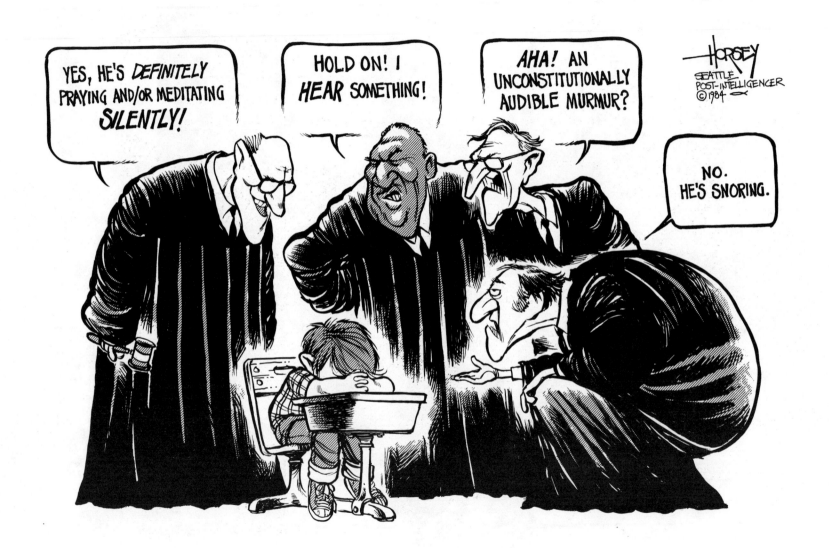

70

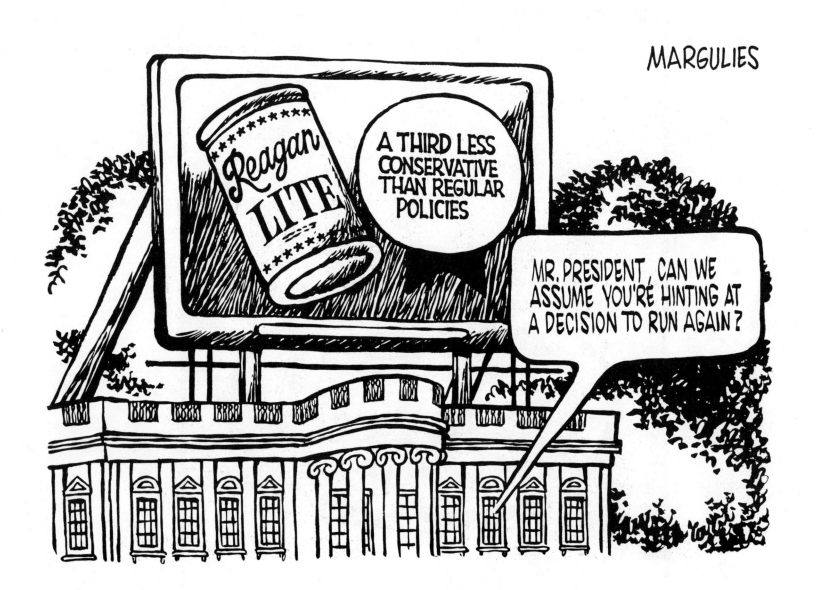

MARGULIES

72

'BUT THE PRESIDENT HAS BEEN REAL NICE ABOUT IT. HE CUT THEIR SOCIAL SECURITY BENEFITS, BUT HE'S ENCOURAGING THEM TO WORK PAST 65... G'NIGHT GRAN'MA.'

79

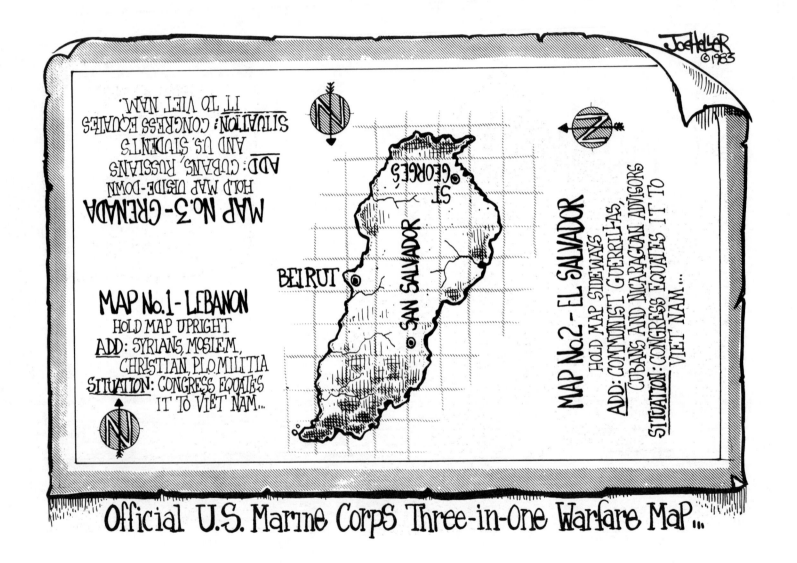

Official U.S. Marine Corps Three-in-One Warfare Map...

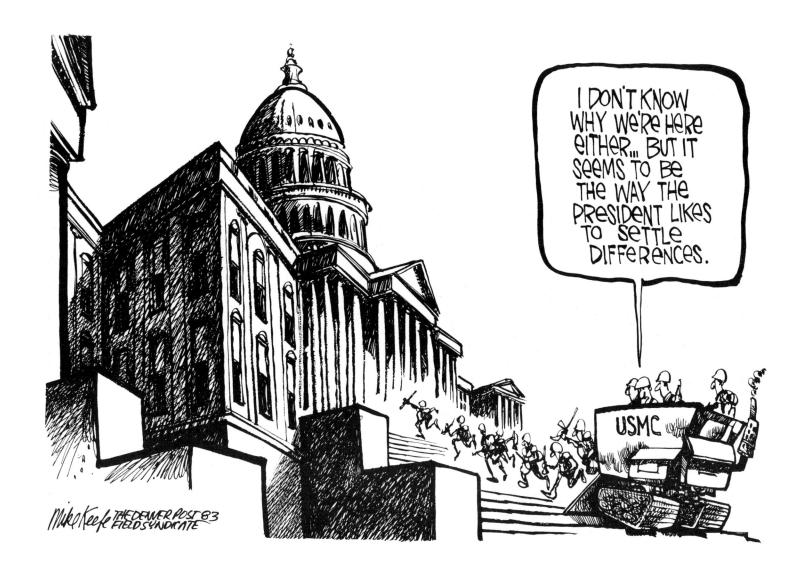

AND THE ROCKETS' RED GLARE, THE BOMBS BURSTING IN AIR,
GAVE PROOF THROUGH THE NIGHT THAT OUR FLAG WAS STILL THERE.

"I propose we reword the First Amendment and make it: FREEDOM FROM THE PRESS."

85

86

'NOW THAT YOU'RE OUT OF WORK, MR. REAGAN WOULD LIKE TO KNOW IF YOU COULD VOLUNTEER FOR SOMETHING'

FEIFFER®

A TRUE LEADER IS WILLING TO GO AGAINST HIS OWN KIND.

, F.D.R. WAS **RICH**. HE DUMPED ON WALL STREET.

IKE WAS A **GENERAL**. HE ATTACKED THE MILITARY- INDUSTRIAL -COMPLEX.

L.B.J. WAS SOUTH- ERN. HE SPONSORED THE VOTING RIGHTS ACT.

I BETCHA THE FIRST **BLACK** PRESIDENT WILL BE AN UNCLE TOM; THE FIRST **WOMAN** PRESIDENT WILL OPPOSE E.R.A.; THE FIRST **JEWISH** PRESIDENT WILL RECOGNIZE THE P.L.O.

I'M THE FIRST **OLD** PRESIDENT.

SOCIAL SECURITY MUST GO.

"GOOD NEWS, SIR... WE JUST RECEIVED A LETTER FROM A GROUP OF TEACHERS WHO SAY THEY'LL WORK FOR MERIT PAY IF YOU WILL TOO..."

TONIGHT'S PROGRAM

GENGHIS KHAN WILL ADDRESS HUMAN RIGHTS ISSUES

BILLY MARTIN WILL GIVE A TALK ON 'SELF CONTROL'

LUCIANO PAVAROTTI WILL SING 'COUNTRY AND WESTERN'

JIM PALMER WILL MODEL FULL LENGTH FURS

JOHN McENROE WILL LECTURE ON MANNERS

RONALD REAGAN WILL SPEAK ON EDUCATION

95

97

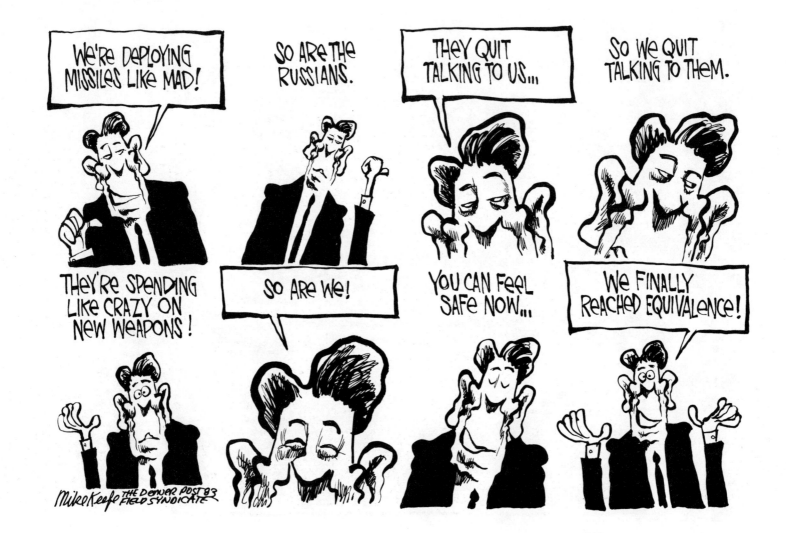

Your Defense Dollar at Work:

STEIN
NEA
ROCKY
MTN.
NEWS
'82

1. Army requests simple, lightweight attack weapon. Est cost: $3.98.

2. Field tests indicate more firepower needed. Est. cost: $186.

3. Marines insist on night version. Est. cost: $17,416.

4. Intelligence suggests it needs armor. Est. cost: $188,749.66.

5. It now requires mobility. $2,115,210.

6. High profile makes it vulnerable. Army requests new support system.

'DENSE' PACK

BRIAN BASSET THE ©1982 SEATTLE TIMES

105

"MY ADVISOR IS DAVID STOCKMAN; AND WHEN DAVID STOCKMAN TALKS..."

Edwin goes to bed hungry every night

His name is Edwin Meese, but you can call him Eddie. Little Eddie has nothing to eat — except his words. You see, Eddie said he's not convinced there are hungry children in America.

For Eddie, Christmas may be just another day full of pain, rejection, hunger. And another mouthful of words.

But with your help, there is hope.

Save Eddie from himself — and from the children. Send your package to:

C.A.R.E. (Climb Aboard Reality, Eddie)
White House
Washington, D.C.

Please don't wait. Somewhere in America, right now, children are going hungry.

SAVE THE CHILDREN FROM EDWIN, INC.

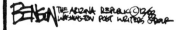

"HE DOESN'T LIKE TO FIDDLE WITH FILLING IN DETAILS, BUT YOU GOTTA ADMIT THE SCALE IS IMPRESSIVE AND THE SIGNATURE IS BOLDLY EXECUTED"

PUTTING A NEW FACE ON U.S. STRATEGY TOWARD THE SOVIET UNION.

109

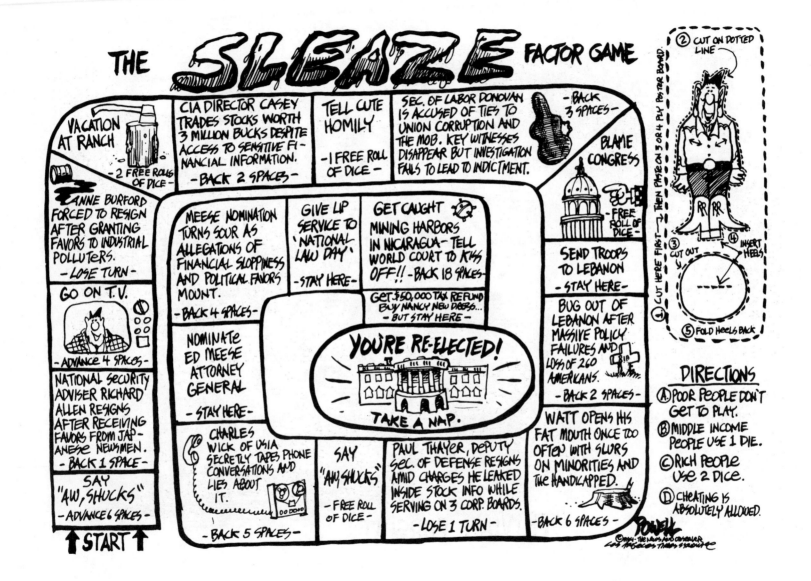

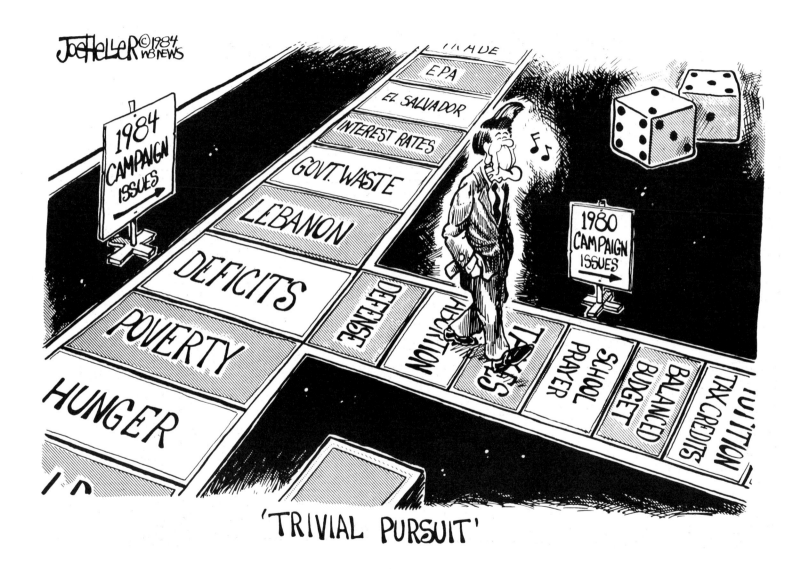

'TRIVIAL PURSUIT'

113

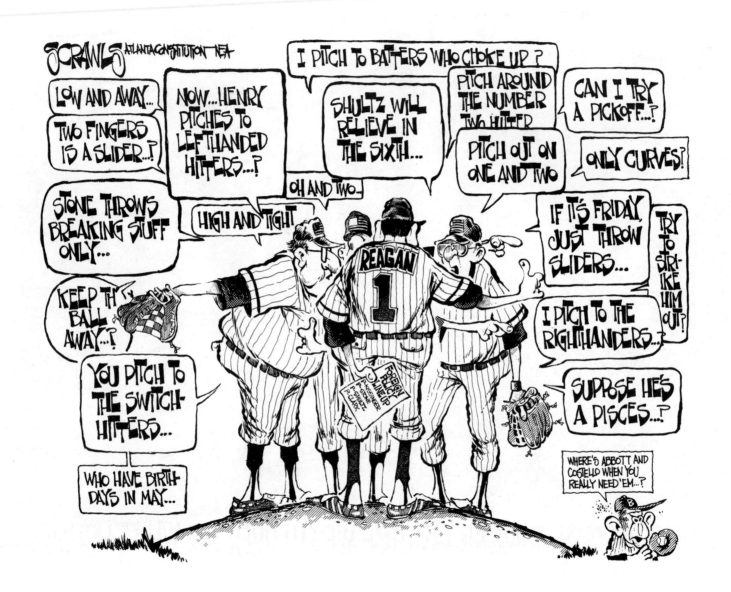

114

I MEAN IT, RUDOLPH.. THAT'S THE LAST TIME WE FLY OVER THE WHITE HOUSE.,

116

MARGULIES

"I'M SUPPORTING REAGAN THIS YEAR BECAUSE HE WANTS TO RETURN THE COUNTRY TO THE WAY THINGS USED TO BE..."

"No, Virginia, There is No Santa Claus."

"WELL NO, I DIDN'T GET TRADE CONCESSIONS BUT I GOT THIS SWELL MODEL OF A TOYOTA CELICA GT"

121

122

'YAWN - GREAT NIGHTS SLEEP! WONDER IF ANYTHING HAPPENED LAST NIGHT?'

124

"CONGRATULATIONS, STOCKMAN... WE FINALLY GOT THE FEDERAL GOVERNMENT DOWN TO THE SIZE WE WANTED!"

WINDOW OF VULNERABILITY

Order Form

To those of you who have enjoyed reading your friend's copy of this book, who would now like to order a copy of your own, but who live far from civilization or its best representative, a bookstore, may we recommend your indulgent Xeroxing of this order form. If you can muster the energy to fill out the facsimile, fold it, stuff it with a check, slip it into a stamped envelope, and trundle it off to your mailbox, we can accomodate you with a mint collector's copy of *Reagancomics*.

Name _____

Street _____

City _____

State _____ Zip _____

☐ Please send post-haste one copy of the splendiferous *Reagancomics*. Price shipped: $7.50.

☐ Please send post-post-haste one copy of *A Nuclear War Would Just Ruin My Day* (a collection of editorial cartoons on the nuclear war threat published simultaneously with *Reagancomics*.) Price shipped: $6.50.

☐ Please send (so that I can have the complete library), one copy of Khyber Press's first title, published in 1983—the audacious *100 Watts: the James Watt Memorial Cartoon Collection*. Price shipped $6.50.

Expect shipment ordinarily within two to three weeks.

Order from:

Khyber Press
P.O. Box 1616
Auburn, WA 98002